Anna Miller

Do Workers' Remittances Bring Economic Growth to Receiving Countries?

A Macro Panel Analysis

GRIN Verlag

Bibliografische Information der Deutschen Nationalbibliothek:

Die Deutsche Bibliothek verzeichnet diese Publikation in der Deutschen National-
bibliografie; detaillierte bibliografische Daten sind im Internet über http://dnb.d-
nb.de/ abrufbar.

Imprint:

Copyright © 2013 GRIN Verlag GmbH
Druck und Bindung: Books on Demand GmbH, Norderstedt Germany
ISBN: 978-3-656-43911-0

GRIN - Your knowledge has value

Der GRIN Verlag publiziert seit 1998 wissenschaftliche Arbeiten von Studenten, Hochschullehrern und anderen Akademikern als eBook und gedrucktes Buch. Die Verlagswebsite www.grin.com ist die ideale Plattform zur Veröffentlichung von Hausarbeiten, Abschlussarbeiten, wissenschaftlichen Aufsätzen, Dissertationen und Fachbüchern.

Visit us on the internet:

http://www.grin.com/

http://www.facebook.com/grincom

http://www.twitter.com/grin_com

The University of Nottingham

School of Economics

Module: L14009 Economic Data Analysis

Do Workers' Remittances Bring Economic Growth to the Receiving Country?
A Macro Panel Analysis

Anna Miller

MSc in Applied Economics and Financial Economics

2012 - 2013

18th January 2013

1 Introduction

Besides foreign direct investment (FDI) and capital market flows, workers' remittances are another external channel for capital flows. According to the OECD, remittances to developing countries amounted to US$ 149.4 billion in the year 2002. However, whereas FDI and capital market flows are subject to variation due to recessions in home countries, remittances are steadily rising every year (OECD, 2006), reaching an amount of about UD$ 300 billion in the year 2007 (Barajas et al., 2009). To give a brief definition, remittances are money transfers from migrants working abroad to their families in their home countries. Yet, the question is, do these remittances contribute to or boost economic growth in receiving countries or are they only a means to increase the migrants' families' welfare by directly reducing their poverty and raising the living standard (Rao and Hassan, 2011). In other words, are remittances mostly used for consumption or do they rather flow in education, and thereby contribute to the human capital, and in investments, thus increasing the capital stock in the economy (Giuliano and Ruiz-Arranz, 2009)? From the growth theory we know that consumption does not have any impact on growth, only investments, either in production or in human capital, can affect long-run growth. Evidence from Indonesia, Ecuador, and Argentina (Sayan, 2006) shows that remittances indirectly reduce volatility of growth of output in times of crises and increase the growth rate thereby (Rao and Hassan, 2011). In contrast, Sayan (2006) found that remittances are moving procyclically with out in recipient countries, boosting incomes during booms, but reducing them even more during recessions and thus magnifying the economic crisis.

This paper examines the relationship between remittances and GDP growth using in a macro panel with 67 countries and a time period of 28 years, from 1975 through 2002, as well as a cross-section analysis for comparison. The goal of this analysis is to determine whether, and to what extent, remittances have an impact on long-term economic growth and, if so, whether this relation is significant or not. The paper is structured as follows. Section 2 briefly gives an overview of the theoretical framework of the growth theory. Section 3 presents and describes the data. Section 4 provides the empirical analyses, consisting of a cross-sectional and panel analysis, and presents the results of these. Section 5 concludes.

2 Idea of the Growth Theory

The following section should provide a short overview of the neoclassical growth theory and especially the exogenous long-run growth model developed by Robert Solow (1956).

The real income is given by $Y(t)$, which is partly spent for consumption and partly saved and invested. Every period a constant fraction s of output is saved, such that the savings rate is $sY(t)$. The capital stock is $K(t)$ and net investment I equals aggregate savings:

$$I = sY(t) = S. \tag{1}$$

Investment raises the capital stock every period, at the same time, a constant share $\delta \in (0; 1)$ of capital depreciates. Thus, the law of motion of capital is:

$$\dot{K} = sY(t) - \delta K. \tag{2}$$

Furthermore, the production function is assumed to have constant returns to scale, using capital and labour as inputs and exogenous technological progress:

$$Y = F(K, AL), \tag{3}$$

where A is the labour-augmenting productivity, i.e. after a while more things can be done, and grows at a constant rate: $\dfrac{\dot{A}}{A} = g_A$. Since population grows exogenously at rate n, the growth rate of raw labour L is n as well. Hence the effective labour, AL, is growing at rate $g_A + n$. Let $\hat{k} \equiv \dfrac{K}{AL}$ be capital per effective unit of labour, and dividing (2) by AL on both sides, we get:

$$\frac{\dot{K}}{AL} = sf(\hat{k}) - \delta \hat{k}. \tag{4}$$

Deriving (4) with respect to K/AL and plugging back into (4), we get the growth rate of capital per unit of effective labour:

$$\dot{\hat{k}} = sf(\hat{k}) - (g_A + n + \delta)\hat{k}. \tag{5}$$

As income per capita is given by $Y/L = Af(\hat{k})$, income per capita grows at rate g_A. Similarly, consumption and capital per capita grow at rate g_A. Total income $Y = ALf(\hat{k})$, as well as total consumption and total capital stock is growing at a rate $g_A + n$.

All in all, it could be shown that changes in investment rate s or in the population growth rate n affect the long-run level of output per worker. Consumption does not contribute to the economy's long-run growth, thus if remittances are supposed have an impact on growth, they will have to be invested to a large part and not spent for consumption.

3   Data

The dataset consists of 67 developing countries[1], which I have chosen on the basis of available data from the sample used by Giuliano and Ruiz-Arranz (2009), for the period 1975 – 2002. The dependent variable is *GDP per capita growth* (in annual %). For the depending variable I use the measure *Workers' Remittances and Compensation of Employees in % of GDP*. Both variables are taken from WDI. The remainder of the control variables is also taken from the WDI, if not otherwise indicated, and is the following:

- *Inflation* – as annual percentage change in consumer price index
- *Openness*[2] – obtaining from the sum of imports and exports as percentage of GDP
- *Population growth*
- *Investments* – as ratio of gross fixed capital formation to GDP
- *Government fiscal balance* – cash surplus/deficit as percentage of GDP
- *Human capital*[3] – as percentage of total population aged 15 and over with a complete second level

Table 1 reports the descriptive statistics of all variables used in this analysis. For the extremes I added the country and the year in parentheses to get a better idea of some country characteristics.

Table 1: Descriptive Statistics

	Mean	N	St. Dev.	Median	Max.	Min.
GDP p.c. growth	1.56	1777	5.05	1.92	21.79 (St. Lucia, 1990)	-28.61 (Nicaragua, 1979)
Inflation	45.76	1579	393.09	9.78	11749.64 (Bolivia, 1985)	-7.80 (Niger, 1991)
Pop. Growth	1.83	1876	1.13	2.03	11.18 (Jordan, 1991)	-2.33 (St. Kitts&Nevis, 1984)
Openness	70.9	1779	42.02	59.08	280.36 (Guyana, 1992)	0 (incl. Jordan, 1975)
Investment	21.59	1718	6.90	20.83	55.39 (St. Kitts&Nevis, 1990)	2.55 (Zimbabwe, 1999)
Rem/GDP	3.37	1466	5.19	1.53	38.37 (Samoa, 1990)	0.000029 (Uruguay, 2001)
Remittances[4]	17707	1478	11344	8554	1.57e+10 (India, 2002)	0 (incl. Venezuela, 1981)
Human Capital	6.66	1631	5.60	5.4	30.3 (Mauritius, 2000)	0.1 (Zimbabwe, 1970s, 80s)

---

[1] see Appendix for the whole sample of countries

[2] Data only for imports and exports in % of GDP from WDI

[3] Data taken from the Barro - Lee (2000) series. It was available for the period 1960 – 2000 only in 5-year intervals, therefore I took over the data for each following 4-year gap, respectively, i.e. the years 1975 – 1979 have the same data, and so on.

[4] Current US$

4   Model and Empirical Analysis

To examine the relationship between remittances and growth of GDP per capita, I proceeded in two different ways. First of all, I split the available period 1975 – 2002 into four 7-year periods in order to examine the short-, medium-, and long-run impact of remittances, and estimate the model by ordinary least squares (OLS). Since a cross-section analysis raises issues like endogeneity, in the sense that more remittances are sent when the growth rate increases, so that the causal direction is not obvious, in a second step I address this problem by using a panel framework. The model to be estimated is based on Giuliano and Ruiz-Arranz' (2009) and is the following:

$$GDPgrowth_{it} = \beta_0 + \beta_1 Rem_{it} + \beta_2 X_{it} + \mu_t + \eta_i + \varepsilon_{it}, \tag{6}$$

where $GDPgrowth_{it}$ is the growth rate of GDP per capita in country i at time t, Rem_{it} is remittances over GDP, X_{it} includes all control variables listed in Section 3, μ_t and η_i are time and country specific effects, respectively, and ε_{it} is the error term. The model is tested under the null hypothesis that β_1 is significantly different from 0.

4.1   Results

The results of the OLS estimation are reported in Table 2. The coefficient for remittances is positive but relatively small and not significant; a 1 unit increase raises growth per capita in average by only 0.07. Investment is positive and highly significant, as is predicted by the theory. A one-unit increase in investment is associated with a 0.223 increase in GDP per capita growth. Both, inflation and population growth have a negative and significant effect on GDP growth, although the coefficient of inflation is almost zero. Surprisingly, human capital does not have any effect on GDP growth, its coefficient is almost nil and insignificant. However, Romer's (1990) model of endogenous growth clearly indicates the significance of human capital for growth. Also openness enters with a negative and insignificant value. Above all, the coefficients seem almost identical over time periods, so that the variables appear to have the same impact in the short- as well as in the long-run, although this is not realistic.

The results of the OLS estimation are quite disappointing, which can be due to lack of data or variables, or the aforementioned issue of endogeneity that may cause a wrong direction of causality, and heterogeneity across countries. Therefore I now test the model using the panel framework. Data series were tested for unit root and it appears that both level and first difference data are stationary, which means there is cross-sectional independence.

Table 3 reports the results of the estimations with pooled OLS (POLS), two-way fixed effects (FE), random effects (RE), mean group estimator (MG Estimator), and common correlated effects MG estimator (CCE MG Estimator).

Comparing the cross-section and panel analysis, one can see one striking result: remittances over GDP are now positive and significant at least on the 5% level in three of five cases (columns (1) – (3)). A one-unit increase in Rem/GDP leads to an increase in GDP p.c. growth by 0.075 (POLS), 0.208 (FE), and

Table 2: Remittances (in % of GDP) and economic growth: cross-section estimation OLS (1975 – 2002)

	(1)	(2)	(3)
	Short-run (1975 – 1981)	Medium-run (1975 – 1995)	Long-run (1975 – 2002)
Inflation	-0.0008**	-0.0008**	-0.0008**
	(-2.47)	(-2.26)	(-2.49)
Pop. Growth	-0.453***	-0.387**	-0.413***
	(-2.91)	(-2.37)	(-2.65)
Openness	-0.0044	-0.0049	-0.0045
	(-1.14)	(-1.24)	(-1.17)
Investment	0.223***	0.223***	0.232***
	(8.93)	(8.94)	(9.47)
Rem/GDP	0.075	0.073	0.069
	(1.96)	(1.89)	(1.81)
Human Capital	0.018	0.001	0.009
	(0.69)	(0.38)	(0.35)
Constant	-2.199***	-2.040***	-2.258***
	(-3.36)	(-3.11)	(-3.46)
Observations	1144	1144	1144
R^2	13.2%	13.8%	12.7%

Notes: Dependent variable is GDP per capita growth. t-statistic is reported in parentheses, * significant at 10%; ** significant at 5%; *** significant at 1%. Time dummies included. Robust standard errors.

0.088 (RE), indicating that remittances are used for investments and are not solely consumed, and actually do contribute to growth. On the other hand, in columns (4) and (5) they are negative and insignificant. When adding $(Rem/GDP)^2$ to the model, the coefficients become insignificant (not reported). This captures the issue that more aid (remittances) has not more effect as long as it is not used efficiently. The results for investment are similar to those in the OLS regression and remain highly significant in all cases except column (5), meaning there is an unambiguous positive effect, an average increase of 0.2 units per one-unit increase, of investments on GDP p.c. growth, irrespective of the methodology.

Furthermore, controlling for fixed effects, many results change significantly comparing with those from the POLS and random effects. Population growth becomes completely insignificant and human capital has a negative, yet also insignificant, effect. Interestingly, remittances have the highest and most significant coefficient (0.208) of those three estimations. Performing a Hausman test, the fixed-effects estimation seems reasonable and consistent with the data. However, there seem to be heterogeneity in remittances over GDP, as its coefficient from the mean group estimator differs a lot from RE and FE.

Table 3: Remittances (in % of GDP) and economic growth: panel estimation (1975 – 2002)

	(1)	(2)	(3)	(4)	(5)
	POLS	FE	RE	MG Estimator	CCE MG Estimator
Inflation	-0.0007***	-0.0007**	-0.0008***	-0.045	-0.0653**
	(-2.72)	(2.40)	(-2.89)	(-1.36)	(-2.04)
Pop. Growth	-0.379***	-0.237	-0.421***	0.06	-2.383
	(-2.61)	(-0.83)	(-2.62)	(0.04)	(-1.37)
Openness	-0.005	-0.0006	-0.004	0.102***	0.046
	(-1.36)	(-0.06)	(-1.01)	(3.64)	(0.96)
Investment	0.233***	0.144***	0.213***	0.151**	0.186
	10.45	(4.50)	(8.87)	(2.14)	(1.81)
Rem/GDP	0.075**	0.208***	0.088**	-1.036	-0.631
	(2.22)	(3.05)	(2.18)	(-1.90)	(-1.98)
Human Capital	0.0007	-0.0521	0.011	0.439	0.559
	(0.02)	(-0.79)	(0.35)	(0.316)	(1.46)
Constant	-1.155	-0.121	-1.918***	-1.07	6.576
	(-0.97)	(-0.08)	(-2.92)	(-0.26)	(0.55)
Observations	1144	1144	1144	1109	1133
R^2	17.2%	9.4%[5]	3.8%		
Root Mean Squared Error				2.8230	2.0085

Notes: Dependent variable is GDP per capita growth. t-statistic is reported in parentheses, * significant at 10%; ** significant at 5%; *** significant at 1%.

As was the case in the cross-section analysis, openness and human capital still do not have any significant effect, except the case using MG estimators, when openness becomes positive and highly significant, again an indicator for heterogeneity in openness.

Although single coefficients from the panel analysis seem to be more significant than in the cross-section analysis, the regressions as a whole are all not significant enough to regard them as relevant. All R-squared are very low, with 17.2% (for POLS) being the highest and the lowest only 3.8% (RE), also the mean root squared errors for MG estimator and CCE MG estimator are quite high with 2.8 and 2, respectively.

5   Concluding remarks

The aim of this paper was to analyse the effect of remittances on GDP per capita growth. Using different estimation methods, I received very divers results. The OLS

---

[5] 'within' R^2 for FE and RE

estimation predicts a positive but insignificant impact of remittances on growth. This may be not only due to insufficient data, but also because a cross-section analysis does not account for endogeneity and heterogeneity between countries. Also other papers dealing with this topic could not find any significant effects with OLS estimation. Significant and positive coefficients could be obtained using a panel analysis. Although even here results differ dramatically. A positive and highly significant effect is provided when controlling for country fixed-effects, whereas MG and CCE MG estimators give negative and insignificant coefficients.

Probably it is not possible to receive one general result for remittances; similar to the case with FDI one should account for different channels of remittances and analyse them separately, let alone the differences in country characteristics. Rao and Hassan (2011) found two channels through which remittances have an indirect effect, namely investment and development of the financial sector. Finally, cyclicality of remittances is also a matter which should be accounted for in examinations of this relationship.

6   References

Barajas, A., Chami, R., Fullenkamp, C., Gapen, M., Montiel, P. *Do Workers' Remittances Promote Economic Growth?* IMF Working Paper (2009).

Barro, R. J. and X. Sala-i-Martin. *Economic Growth*. Second Edition. Cambridge: MIT Press, 2004.

Giuliano, P., Ruiz-Arranz, M. *Remittances, Financial Development, and Growth*. Journal of Development Economics 90 (2009): 144–152.

OECD. *International Migrant Remittances and Their Role in Development*. International Migration Outlook: Sopemi 2006 Edition.

Rao, B., Hassan, G. *A Panel Data Analysis of the Growth Effects of Remittances*. Economic Modelling 28 (2011): 701–709.

Sayan, S. *Business Cycles and Workers' Remittances: How Do Migrant Workers Respond to Cyclical Movements of GDP at Home?* IMF Working Paper (2006).

Appendix

Countries in the sample

Argentina	Guyana	Nepal	South Africa
Barbados	Honduras	Nicaragua	Sri lanka
Benin	Hungary	Niger	St. Kitts and Nevis
Bolivia	India	Pakistan	St. Lucia
Botswana	Indonesia	Panama	Sudan
Brazil	Iran, Islamic Rep.	Paraguay	Swaziland
Cameroon	Jamaica	Peru	Syrian Arab Republic
Chile	Jordan	Philippines	Thailand
China	Kenya	Poland	Togo
Colombia	Malawi	Romania	Tonga
Costa rica	Malaysia	Russian Federation	Trinidad and Tobago
Domonica	Mali	Samoa	Tunisia
Domenican Republic	Malta	Senegal	Turkey
Ecuador	Mauritania	Seychelles	Uruguay
Egypt	Mauritius	Sierra Leone	Venezuela, RB
El Salvador	Mexico	Slovak Republic	Zimbabwe
Guatemala	Mozambique	Slovenia	

Main STATA output from estimation of equation (6)

POLS

```
. xi: reg YpcGrowth inflation remgdp HumanCapital Investment Openness PopGrowth i.year
i.year          _Iyear_1975-2002    (naturally coded; _Iyear_1975 omitted)

      Source |       SS       df       MS              Number of obs =     1144
-------------+------------------------------           F( 33,  1110) =     6.99
       Model | 3927.66031      33  119.020009           Prob > F      =   0.0000
    Residual | 18891.566     1110  17.0194288           R-squared     =   0.1721
-------------+------------------------------           Adj R-squared =   0.1475
       Total | 22819.2263    1143  19.9643275           Root MSE      =   4.1255

------------------------------------------------------------------------------
   YpcGrowth |      Coef.   Std. Err.      t    P>|t|     [95% Conf. Interval]
-------------+----------------------------------------------------------------
   inflation |  -.000756    .000278    -2.72   0.007    -.0013015   -.0002106
      remgdp |  .0753091    .0339545     2.22   0.027     .0086869    .1419313
 HumanCapital |  .0006682    .0270169     0.02   0.980    -.0523418    .0536781
  Investment |  .2328717    .0222787    10.45   0.000     .1891585    .2765849
    Openness |  -.0048923    .0035994    -1.36   0.174    -.0119547    .0021701
   PopGrowth |  -.3786659    .1449366    -2.61   0.009    -.6630466   -.0942852
  _Iyear_1976 |  .7470389    1.356197     0.55   0.582     -1.91396    3.408038
  _Iyear_1977 |  -.1230468    1.293580    -0.10   0.924    -2.661203    2.415109
  _Iyear_1978 |  -.5135462    1.286483    -0.40   0.690    -3.037759    2.010667
  _Iyear_1979 |  -1.138113    1.264766    -0.90   0.368    -3.619715    1.343489
  _Iyear_1980 |  -.5202567    1.258032    -0.41   0.679    -2.988645    1.948132
  _Iyear_1981 |  -1.440189    1.246699    -1.16   0.248    -3.886342    1.005964
  _Iyear_1982 |  -3.678988    1.246052    -2.95   0.003     -6.12387   -1.234105
  _Iyear_1983 |  -3.916897    1.240824    -3.16   0.002    -6.351521   -1.482272
  _Iyear_1984 |  -2.518146    1.235782    -2.04   0.042    -4.942879   -.0934129
  _Iyear_1985 |  -1.803275    1.245958    -1.45   0.148    -4.247973    .6414229
  _Iyear_1986 |  -.991664    1.237059    -0.80   0.423    -3.418902    1.435574
  _Iyear_1987 |  -.3041151    1.226555    -0.25   0.804    -2.710743    2.102513
  _Iyear_1988 |  -.4722492    1.221905    -0.39   0.699    -2.869754    1.925256
  _Iyear_1989 |  -.9921231    1.21783     -0.81   0.415    -3.381631    1.397384
  _Iyear_1990 |  -1.61907    1.212677    -1.34   0.182    -3.998468    .7603276
  _Iyear_1991 |  -1.096503    1.214325    -0.90   0.367    -3.479134    1.286128
  _Iyear_1992 |  -.9648599    1.214527    -0.79   0.427    -3.347888    1.418169
  _Iyear_1993 |  -1.434691    1.199751    -1.20   0.232    -3.788727    .9193453
  _Iyear_1994 |  -.9591308    1.184084    -0.81   0.418    -3.282427    1.364165
  _Iyear_1995 |  -.0965693    1.183082    -0.08   0.935    -2.417899    2.224761
  _Iyear_1996 |  -.2926882    1.183225    -0.25   0.805    -2.614298    2.028922
  _Iyear_1997 |  -.0257921    1.183353    -0.02   0.983    -2.347653    2.296069
  _Iyear_1998 |  -1.760963    1.186237    -1.48   0.138    -4.088484    .5665575
  _Iyear_1999 |  -1.543130    1.18791     -1.30   0.194    -3.873941    .7876637
  _Iyear_2000 |  -.6369051    1.186173    -0.54   0.591    -2.964299    1.690489
  _Iyear_2001 |  -1.722028    1.185786    -1.45   0.147    -4.048663    .604606
  _Iyear_2002 |  -1.205597    1.190585    -1.01   0.311    -3.541648    1.130454
       _cons |  -1.154974    1.188136    -0.97   0.331     -3.48622    1.176271
------------------------------------------------------------------------------
```

Fixed Effects

```
. xi: xtreg YpcGrowth inflation PopGrowth Openness Investment remgdp HumanCapital i.year, fe
i.year          _Iyear_1975-2002    (naturally coded; _Iyear_1975 omitted)
```

```
Fixed-effects (within) regression              Number of obs      =      1144
Group variable: id                             Number of groups   =        58

R-sq:  within  = 0.0939                         Obs per group: min =         1
       between = 0.3389                                        avg =      19.7
       overall = 0.1376                                        max =        28

                                               F(33,1053)         =      3.31
corr(u_i, Xb)  = 0.0041                         Prob > F           =    0.0000
```

YpcGrowth	Coef.	Std. Err.	t	P>|t|	[95% Conf. Interval]	
inflation	-.0006817	.0002842	-2.40	0.017	-.0012394	-.0001239
PopGrowth	-.237009	.2869522	-0.83	0.409	-.8000723	.3260542
Openness	-.0006219	.0097534	-0.06	0.949	-.0197602	.0185164
Investment	.1440972	.0319894	4.50	0.000	.081327	.2068674
remgdp	.2078415	.0681447	3.05	0.002	.0741266	.3415564
HumanCapital	-.0520846	.0659117	-0.79	0.430	-.1814178	.0772486

Random Effects

```
. xtreg YpcGrowth inflation PopGrowth Openness Investment remgdp HumanCapital , re
```

```
Random-effects GLS regression                  Number of obs      =      1144
Group variable: id                             Number of groups   =        58

R-sq:  within  = 0.0381                         Obs per group: min =         1
       between = 0.5613                                        avg =      19.7
       overall = 0.1269                                        max =        28

Random effects u_i ~ Gaussian                   Wald chi2(6)       =    120.61
corr(u_i, X)      = 0 (assumed)                 Prob > chi2        =    0.0000
```

YpcGrowth	Coef.	Std. Err.	z	P>|z|	[95% Conf. Interval]	
inflation	-.0008012	.0002773	-2.89	0.004	-.0013447	-.0002577
PopGrowth	-.4208512	.1607973	-2.62	0.009	-.7360082	-.1056942
Openness	-.00438	.0043517	-1.01	0.314	-.0129091	.0041492
Investment	.2132411	.024031	8.87	0.000	.1661413	.2603409
remgdp	.0880205	.0404367	2.18	0.029	.008766	.167275
HumanCapital	.0109233	.0310694	0.35	0.725	-.0499715	.0718182
_cons	-1.918375	.6568177	-2.92	0.003	-3.205714	-.6310363
sigma_u	.71369214					
sigma_e	4.1171163					
rho	.02917276	(fraction of variance due to u_i)				

10

Mean Group Estimator

```
. xtmg YpcGrowth inflation remgdp PopGrowth Openness HumanCapital Investment , trend robust res(eMG)
  Note: 35 obs. dropped (panels too small)
```

Pesaran & Smith (1995) Mean Group estimator

All coefficients present represent averages across groups (**id**)
Coefficient averages computed as **outlier-robust** means (using rreg)

Mean Group type estimation			Number of obs	=	1109
Group variable: **id**			Number of groups	=	51
			Obs per group: min =		9
			avg =		21.7
			max =		28
			Wald chi2(**6**)	=	24.30
			Prob > chi2	=	0.0005

YpcGrowth	Coef.	Std. Err.	z	P>|z|	[95% Conf. Interval]	
inflation	-.0453771	.0332643	-1.36	0.173	-.110574	.0198197
remgdp	-1.036312	.5450076	-1.90	0.057	-2.104587	.0318832
PopGrowth	.060499	1.506437	0.04	0.968	-2.895982	3.01696
Openness	.1821788	.0280946	3.64	0.000	.0471144	.1572432
HumanCapital	.4396739	.4384107	1.00	0.316	-.4195952	1.298943
Investment	.1508138	.0703723	2.14	0.032	.0128867	.2887409
_000007_t	-.0878109	.1190513	-0.74	0.461	-.3211472	.1455253
_cons	-12.00478	6.239974	-1.92	0.054	-24.23491	.2253399

Root Mean Squared Error (sigma): **2.8230**
(RMSE uses residuals from group-specific regressions: unaffected by 'robust').
Residual series based on country regressions stored in variable: **eMG**
Variable **__000007_t** refers to a group-specific linear trend.
Share of group-specific trends significant at 5% level: **0.098 (= 5 trends)**

Common Correlated Effects MG estimator

```
. xtmg YpcGrowth inflation remgdp Investment Openness PopGrowth HumanCapital , robust res(eCMG) cce
  Note: 11 obs. dropped (panels too small)
```

Pesaran (2006) Common Correlated Effects Mean Group estimator

All coefficients present represent averages across groups (**id**)
Coefficient averages computed as **outlier-robust** means (using rreg)

Mean Group type estimation			Number of obs	=	1133
Group variable: **id**			Number of groups	=	54
			Obs per group: min =		8
			avg =		21.0
			max =		28
			Wald chi2(**6**)	=	16.28
			Prob > chi2	=	0.0123

YpcGrowth	Coef.	Std. Err.	z	P>|z|	[95% Conf. Interval]	
inflation	-.0653094	.0319573	-2.04	0.041	-.1279445	-.0026743
remgdp	-.6308656	.3193432	-1.98	0.048	-1.256767	-.0049645
Investment	.1856414	.10239	1.81	0.070	-.0150393	.386322
Openness	.0454913	.0475496	0.96	0.339	-.0477042	.1386868
PopGrowth	-2.383003	1.740047	-1.37	0.171	-5.793433	1.027427
HumanCapital	.559767	.3846084	1.46	0.146	-.1940516	1.313586
__00000M_Y~h	1.061588	.2925271	3.63	0.000	.4882452	1.63493
__00000L_i~n	.0005433	.0026871	0.20	0.840	-.0047233	.00581
__00000L_r~p	-.1039368	.5577082	-0.19	0.852	-1.197025	.9891512
__00000L_I~t	.2048832	.2344939	0.87	0.382	-.2547164	.6644828
__00000L_O~s	-.2527194	.1110623	-2.28	0.023	-.4703976	-.0350413
__00000L_P~h	-.186234	1.305087	-0.14	0.887	-2.744157	2.371689
__00000L_H~l	-.5272754	.2706791	-1.95	0.051	-1.057797	.0032459
_cons	6.576366	11.92928	0.55	0.581	-16.80459	29.95733

Root Mean Squared Error (sigma): **2.0085**
(RMSE uses residuals from group-specific regressions: unaffected by 'robust').
Cross-section averaged **regressors** are marked by the suffix:
    _YpcGrowth, _inflation, _remgdp, _Investment, _Openness, _PopGrowth, _HumanCapital respectively.
Residual series based on country regressions stored in variable: **eCMG**